How it all began...

Our world is wonderful. Some people come up with theories of how it came about. Let's remember that our God is the Creator of it all. And that when he made it, it was perfect. God himself said that it was good!

The creation of the world took place over six days with an additional day for rest at the end. Here we look at these seven days as our artist portrays them...

Day One: On the very first day God created light and darkness. God decided to call the light day and the darkness he decided to call night.

Day Two: On the second day God made the sky.

Day Three: God took some of the water to one place so there would be a dry area. He called this dry area land.

Then God made plants, flowers and trees.

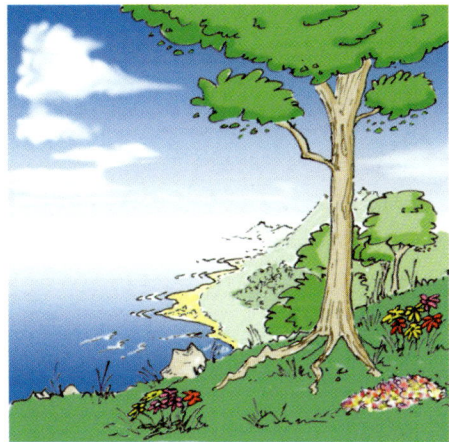

Day Four: The sun was made on this day. God also made the moon and stars so that the night would not be too dark.

Continued on page 4

Day Five: God made the birds and the fish on this day.

Day Six: What a wonderful day. On this day all the animals were made. The giraffe, camel, chimpanzee, tortoise, lion, elephant, polar bear and panda. Countless numbers of animals. Some animals that no longer exist and some animals that

are still to be discovered. God made them all. God also made man. The first man's name was Adam. But that wasn't all he made. God also made the first woman and her name was Eve.

Day Seven: The seventh day came and God declared that this was to be a day of rest and nothing else was made.

Next article: Read about how it all went wrong (page 5). The worst disaster this world has ever faced. Find out how this disaster effects you. (page 6)

What's What?

Adam: Adam is the first man who was created. The very first human being to exist. He was made by God and was created in the image of God.

Eve: Eve is the first woman who was created. She was also made by God as a friend and companion for Adam.

Eden: This is the name for the garden where Adam and Eve lived. Adam and Eve both lived happily in the garden of Eden until sin entered their lives. Because of their sin they were banished from the garden.

HOW IT ALL WENT WRONG!

Our world is a wonderful world.

However, this world is full of pain and suffering and many horrible things. Human beings are destroying God's world and each other. Our special report continues with - *How it all went wrong!* It is the worst disaster our world has ever known.

God's enemy the devil hated the beautiful world God had created. He hated the fact that God had made human beings happy in this perfect world. So he disguised himself as a serpent and waited for Eve to walk by.

Tricked !

He then asked Eve 'Did God really say that you must not eat from any tree in the garden?' Eve replied, 'God has said that we must not eat of the tree that is in the middle of the garden, and we must not touch it, or we will die.' The serpent deceived Eve, 'You won't really die. God knows that when you eat from that tree your eyes will be opened and you will be like God, knowing good and evil.'

Eve looked at the fruit, saw it was good and believed what the serpent said. She ate it.

(continued on page 6)

Eve also gave some to her husband, Adam, and he ate it.

Tricked again!

Too late, they realised they had been tricked by the serpent. They had disobeyed God and would be punished. They had to leave the garden of Eden - never to return.

GOOD NEWS FLASH!!

Thankfully God had a rescue plan.

He told Adam and Eve that there would be a second chance. God promised that one day sin and the devil would be crushed and that a rescuer would come to save people from their sins.

Throughout the years God spoke to those who trusted him. He told them about the rescuer who would come to save them. Many years later - Jesus Christ was born in Bethlehem. He was God's son, the rescuer, the Saviour. He took our punishment instead of us when he died on the cross.

All we have to do is to trust in Jesus. That is how you get right with God. Ask God to help you. Speak to him -

Just like Enoch!

some people call that prayer. Learn about God by spending time with him and by reading his book - The Bible.

Boat made ready to sail on dry land!

An amazing sight - Artist's depiction of eye witness accounts.

You may have heard people talking about a time when a flood covered the earth. We can report just what happened all those years ago.

Many years ago a man named Noah lived on the earth. He was good and loved and obeyed God. All the other people at that time did bad things and God was not happy. He told Noah that he was going to destroy the earth and all the bad things in it. 'You must build a special boat called an ark and get ready because the flood is coming.'

God gave exact instructions on how the ark was to be built. It was to be a certain size with three floors. Noah was to take his family and two of every kind of animal into the ark as well as enough food for them all.

... Noah had to put up with a lot of jokes...

It would appear that Noah had to put up with a lot of jokes being made at him by those who saw him. There he was building a boat and there was

(continued on page 8)

no water nearby. Eventually the boat was ready and the family and animals went in. When the doors closed the rain began. It rained and rained and, outside the ark everything was destroyed. But Noah and everything in the ark was safe.

Everything destroyed!

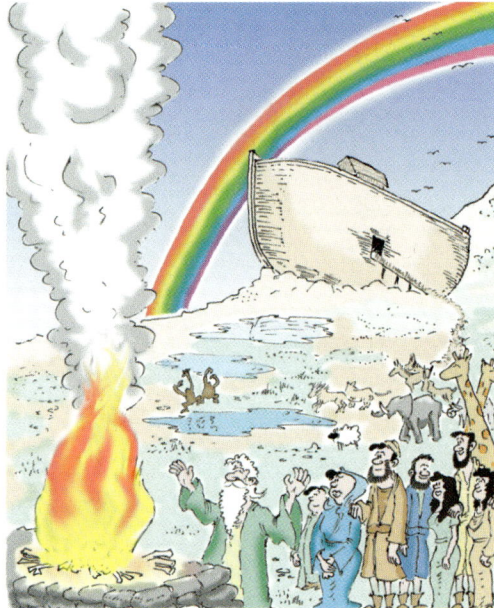

Once the water went down they all got out and Noah made an altar to God.

This pleased God and he promised not to flood the earth again. As a sign of this promise God put a rainbow in the sky.

Now every time we see a rainbow it can help us to remember how God saved Noah and of God's great love for us.

New wonder lights up sky - A rainbow!

ARK PROFILE: **Architect - God   Chief Builder - Noah**

The ark was: 450 feet long, 75 feet wide, 45 feet high.
There were three floors or decks - upper, middle and lower.
The ark had a roof, a door and at least one window that we know of.
This window could be opened and shut.
The wood that was used in the construction was cypress wood.
The ark was to be coated with pitch (a tar like substance) inside and out.

EGYPT HIT BY TIME OF TERROR

from our Egyptian Correspondent

Egypt has experienced some dreadful problems.

Moses apparently has tried to persuade Pharaoh to let the Israelite people go free. However Pharaoh does not want to loose his slaves but so many bad things have been happening that it looks like they may gain their freedom at last.

Freedom at last!

When Pharaoh first refused, Moses used his stick to hit the waters of the river Nile and then it turned to blood. Imagine blood to wash in... to drink... and what a smell it was - unbearable!

No sooner were people getting over that when frogs started to appear. Frogs can be very nice in a pond or a lake, but in your bed or cooking pots is a different matter.

Frogs and more frogs

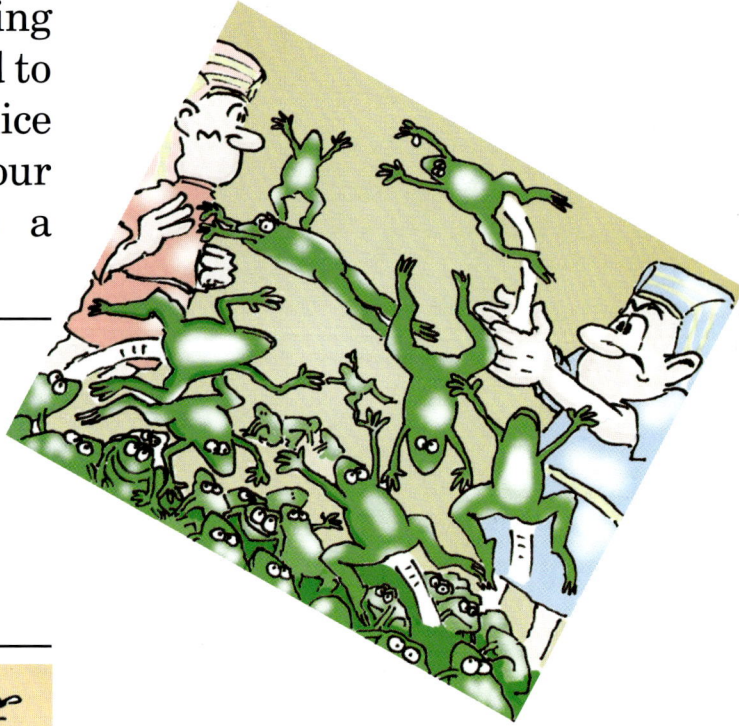

Pharaoh's magicians made even more frogs appear. There was no escaping them. When Pharaoh said the people could go, God let the frogs die... then Pharaoh changed his mind. The slaves were to stay! Next gnats and flies appeared everywhere, they were very annoying.

Gnats! Flies! Boils!

Pharaoh appeared to change his mind but changed it back again!

Then the animals began to die. The horses, donkeys, sheep, goats and cattle belonging to the Egyptians all died while the Israelite's cattle weren't harmed at all. When that didn't bring freedom Moses threw soot in the air and boils broke out on the skin of the Egyptian people. They were in such pain, but still Pharaoh would not grant freedom.

Moses warned Pharaoh that God would send a great hail storm if he didn't let the people go. The storm came, the worst ever. There was thunder, and lightning and hail fell thick and fast. Crops were flattened and trees stripped. But it did not touch the land where God's people were. Pharaoh agreed to let them go, but at the last minute changed his mind.

destroy. Everything was turned black because of the thick cloud of buzzing insects.

Total darkness!

For the next three days God sent darkness on the land but the Israelites had light. God

How unsettling for everyone. This meant that another terror was on it's way. It began like a

Great cloud of locusts!

wind but it was a huge storm of locusts that came over the land and ate anything that the hail had not managed to

was not angry with the Israelites. Then Pharaoh said that the Israelites could go - but he changed his mind yet again. Everyone wonders what else can happen. Will Pharaoh ever let the Israelites go?

STOP PRESS

We are receiving reports that the slaves seem to be making preparations for a journey, will they be allowed to go now?

There is talk that there will be a death tonight in every Egyptian family. The eldest boy is doomed to die because Pharaoh will not let the slaves go. Life is scary! We will keep you up to date as events unfold.

SEVERAL DAYS LATER

It has finally happened, the Israelites are free. But only after death came to each Egyptian family as predicted. Only the Israelites were saved.

Grieving Egyptian families say that every first born in every Egyptian family is dead. Even the animals have been affected. The Israelite families escaped the tragedy and are preparing to depart. They escaped because they obeyed God's instructions to them.

God told the Israelites that the angel of death would avoid their houses if they marked their door frames with blood. Each family had to kill a lamb and paint the tops and sides of

their doors with the blood. They were not to leave their houses until the next morning. That night there was great

Escape

distress in the land of Egypt. There wasn't a house in Egypt that hadn't lost someone.

Israelites get ready to leave.

The Israelite families are now well away from Egypt but even the tragedy of death didn't stop Pharaoh. Pharaoh told his men to chase them and recapture them.

As Moses led the Israelites to the Red Sea it looked as though they had no way forward. However God protects his people in amazing ways. The waters parted and the Israelites got through.

God is amazing!

God confused the Egyptian army. He caused the wheels of their chariots to fall off and when they also tried to cross the Red Sea God told Moses to stretch out his hand again. As he did so the waters of the Red Sea returned to where they had come from. The entire army was drowned. Not one survived. Never has such a time as this been known in the land of Egypt.

(Special report on page 16.)

Hi readers! Thanks for all your letters this week. In this week's problem page I will try and help you to solve your problems... with the help of some well known people from the scriptures. I hope you all get your reply soon.

Uncle Josh

Picture: Lydia

Dear Uncle Josh,

Did Jesus really say that we shouldn't worry about what we are going to eat, drink and wear? How can he say this? I've never heard anything like it!

Confused

Dear Confused,

Yes he did! Jesus knows that God loves to give us what we need. God cares for his people. He fed the Israelites in the desert and even rescued them from the Egyptian army! God can do anything! Lydia, a well known Christian from Thyatira, trusted in God... but she also gave back to God. We should remember to worship and praise God like Lydia did and to share God's gifts to us with other people.

God promises to give us what we need not everything we want. So don't go to God with a great big wish list. We should thank God every day for all the wonderful things he gives us. Try counting out a few of these gifts. You'll be surprised how many you have.

Uncle Josh

Our problem page today refers to various scriptures here are just a few:

Philippians 4:6;
Matthew 6: 25-34;
1 Samuel 17;
Romans 3:23.

Dear Uncle Josh,

I have a problem. I am being bullied by some horrible people. I don't know what to do.

Very scared

Picture: Jochabed

Dear Very scared,

Speak to someone you trust - perhaps a teacher or parent. Ask them to help you. This is very important.

Ask God to help you. Jesus knows what it is like to be hurt by other people. He can give you courage. God gave Jochabed great courage when she hid her baby, Moses, from Pharaoh. Remember to ask a grown up to help you and also ask God.

Uncle Josh

Dear Uncle Josh

I have a problem. I am a really nasty person. I bully other people. I don't know how to stop? Can you help me?

I am sorry

Picture: Zacchaeus

Dear I am sorry,

I'm glad you realise you've done wrong. The only person who can help you is God. Ask him to forgive you. Ask him to help you to be a better person and take control of your life. Everybody needs to do this because we all do wrong things. There is a name for people like us - we are called sinners. Only Jesus Christ has never sinned and so only he can help you to live a life that pleases God.

Do you remember Zacchaeus? He was a bully too but when he met Jesus Christ he felt the same way you do. He felt sorry. Jesus forgave him and Zacchaeus started to put things right. He even gave back the money he'd stolen from people. If you feel you can you should tell the people you have been nasty to that you are sorry. Perhaps they will forgive you and be your friends. Perhaps they wont. God definitely wants to be your friend so say thank you to him now and start a new life with him.

Uncle Josh

Hundreds walk through wall of water!

An amazing event occurred recently when the Israelites were escaping from Egypt.

They made their way through the desert with the Egyptians in hot pursuit. When they put up their tents by the Red Sea they heard that Pharaoh had changed his mind and had sent his army to recapture them. They were terrified. They did not know what to do. The sea was in front of them. There was no way to escape. Many thought they were about to die.

People cried and shouted that they would rather suffer in Egypt than be here. Moses didn't know what to do. Then he heard God's voice. Moses was to tell the people to move

on. God would move the water out of the way. Can you imagine it? As Moses stretched out his hand over the Red Sea a strong East wind began to blow. All that night the wind blew on the Red Sea.

Blow wind blow!

The wind blew the sea to the sides and cleared the way for all the people to walk through. The water was like walls on either side of the Israelites as they walked through to safety.

The Egyptians charged on and at just the right time they were thrown into confusion by first a cloud and then the waters rolling back into place.

Safety

No Egyptian Soldier survived to tell the tale. After this incredible event the faith of the Israelites in God was strengthened and they trusted God even more.

Raining food in the desert

We have told you the story of the wall of water and how God took his people safely through the Red Sea. Well, the adventures of these people just went on and on. Our investigations show us that once they were through the waters and safe, they began to worry because there was nothing for them to eat or drink.

What! No food?

God promised to look after them but they were finding it hard to believe.

Before long they came to a place called Elim where there were springs of water which they could drink from and trees to give them some shelter.

As they moved through the desert though they grumbled more and more because they had no food. Some said that they would rather be back in Egypt where there was food. They forgot the bad times they'd had there. They thought they were about to starve....

God did not forget them

though. He told Moses that he would send bread from heaven. It would come at night and in the morning everyone would collect what they needed for that day. They were not to collect any more, only on the sixth day they were to collect extra so they would have enough for the day of rest.

Yuck! Maggots!

Sadly some people did not listen to the instructions and gathered too much. It went bad and filled up with maggots.

Still the people grumbled. Even though God provided them with plenty food, they

---

Israelite Menu

***

**Quail:
Roasted, boiled or fried**

***

Manna

***

Water to drink

---

were not happy. God then told Moses that quail would also be sent for the people to eat. Quail are small brown birds. God sent the quail in a big rush. The birds just fell out of the sky. Some people talk about raining cats and dogs. Well for the Israelites it was raining small brown birds - everywhere. They soon had plenty to eat.

The Israelites must have learned to enjoy manna because they ate it for another forty years until they arrived at their new land Canaan.

Water supply was another problem. Sometimes they quarrelled with Moses about this. God told Moses to use his staff and hit a nearby rock with it. When he did, water came out for them to drink.

******

The Israelites often thought they couldn't cope but God was always ready to help if they asked him to. This is the same for us today. He is always there for us, we just need to talk to him.

(Special feature on page 20.)

Special Feature

The Maker's Instructions

Hello again readers, isn't it amazing that God has given his people a set of instructions - The Ten Commandments. They are such an important part of our history that we can never be reminded of them too often. We need to remember them and use them everyday in our lives. We print them out again for you here.

10 Commandments

1	Have no gods except me.	6	Do not murder.
2	Do not make any idols.	7	Do not take someone else's wife.
3	Do not use God's name in a wrong way.	8	Do not steal.
4	Keep Sunday special.	9	Do not tell lies.
5	Respect your father and your mother.	10	Do not be jealous.

Did you know that God had to write these commands on two big bits of stone? He even had to do it twice.

It all happened because the people were very bad. God had told Moses to climb a big mountain so he could tell Moses how people were to live to bring glory to his name.

Sadly, while Moses was up on the mountain the people got

Moses smashes the stones.

Obey God's rules!

fed up and began to do bad things that did not please God. When Moses came down and discovered this he was so upset that he smashed the stones with the words on them that God had given him. Later Moses had to go back to God and ask for his forgiveness for the people for what they had done. The commands also had to be written out again.

Let's make sure that we try to follow God's commands.

Fact Box

Jesus is the only one who kept God's law perfectly. He was sinless. Once he was asked 'Which is the most important commandment?'

He gave a very wise reply,

'Love the Lord your God with all your heart and soul and mind and strength.'
Mark 12:30-31

While you have been reading all about the Israelites and their escape from the land of Egypt perhaps you have been wondering what they were doing there in the first place? Where did they come from?

Had they always lived in Egypt? The following two articles come from our Egyptian archives. They report on the amazing story of a young man called Joseph and his rise to political greatness in the land of Egypt.

PRISONER GETS PROMOTION

Pharaoh, has had some strange dreams. None of the wise men could explain the meaning of his dreams to him. No-one knew what to do. Eventually his cupbearer told Pharaoh about what had happened to him two years ago.

He had been in prison and had had a strange dream. Another prisoner told him its meaning and what he had said actually happened. The cupbearer was released and promised to help this man.

Sadly he forgot all about him until now. Pharaoh then fetched this man from prison. His name is Joseph.

Joseph

Joseph admitted that he could not explain the dream but that God would help him. Pharaoh told Joseph about his two dreams. In one he had seen seven thin cows eating up seven fat cows and in the other seven thin ears of corn swallowed up seven full ears of corn. Joseph said that he believed that God was telling Pharaoh that his country was going to have seven good years

Famine

of harvest followed by seven bad years. He advised the king to find a wise person to organise the crops so that in the good years enough would be stored to feed people in the bad years. Pharaoh decided that as God had shown all this to Joseph then Joseph ought to be in charge. Only Pharaoh was to be more important than Joseph. The king gave him his own ring, fine clothes, a gold chain and let him ride in a chariot. Quite a change from life in a prison cell.

BULLIED BOY SOLD AS SLAVE

We recently reported on Egypt's new man at the top. Today we bring you some background knowledge to this man who has risen rapidly to one of the top posts in our land.

He comes from the land of Canaan where he used to live with his family. While he was a boy he himself had strange dreams which God told him the meaning of.

Joseph in charge.

Joseph in the pit.

He had a dream!

His many brothers did not like him because of this and would turn against him.

On one occasion his brothers had gone to look for grazing for the flocks and after a few days the father sent Joseph off to see how the brothers were doing. When they saw him coming they decided that this was their chance to get rid of him. Some thought that they should kill him while one thought to dump him in a pit and then come back for him later.

What rotters!

The brothers did put him in a pit but when some Ishmaelites came by they thought, 'Here is a chance to make some money!' They sold their own brother as a slave and Joseph was taken to Egypt.

Joseph worked for a while before, due to a misunderstanding with his master Potipher, he found himself in prison. Potipher's wife was angry with Joseph so had decided to accuse him of a crime he did not commit.

Potipher threw Joseph into jail where he was left to rot.

But as it happens, wherever he seemed to go it was clear that God was with him in all that he did.

We wish Joseph every success in his new job and hope that he can save us all from starving.

Fact Box: *A slave is someone who is owned by another person. They have no rights or freedoms. Joseph was a good worker and a valued slave. Potipher gave Joseph a lot of responsibility in his house. If it hadn't been for Potipher's wife Joseph would have not been put in jail. However, if Joseph had not been in Jail he would not have finally met with the great Pharaoh. God's plans always work out for the best.*

(There is a mystery to solve on page 26.)

So there is the connection... Joseph. He was an ancestor of the Israelites who became slaves in Egypt. The next story shows how Joseph's powerful position in Egypt led to the rest of his family making Egypt their home.

MYSTERY VISITORS AT PALACE

More news about Joseph, Pharaoh's prime minister.

Visitors were seen leaving his official residence but no one knows who they are. Many foreigners come to Egypt for food as we were not caught off guard by the famine - thanks to Joseph. Joseph's reaction when he saw these visitors was different to usual.

Surprise! Surprise!

Joseph seemed to recognise them but then he spoke harshly to them.

'Where are you from?'

'Canaan' they replied.

You've guessed it - they were Joseph's brothers. They had come to ask for grain - but didn't realise that the important man was their brother Joseph.

Joseph said they were spies which they denied strongly. They mentioned their younger brother Benjamin who was at

Joseph meets his brothers.

home with his father. Benjamin had been Joseph's favourite brother. He longed to see him again. So he ordered that one brother should remain a prisoner while the others returned home with grain. They could return for more grain and to free the prisoner if, next time, they brought Benjamin with them.

Reunion!

The brothers said to each other, 'We are being punished for our treatment of Joseph.'

Benjamin

Joseph then began to cry and turned away incase his brothers started to ask questions. Simeon was then tied up and the grain given out.

When the brothers returned Joseph saw Benjamin. He cried so much he had to leave the room. He then gave a large banquet for his brothers. They were amazed when they sat down at the table. They were all seated in order of their ages and Benjamin got much more food than anyone else.

Later Joseph told a servant to hide his silver cup in Benjamin's sack. It looked as though Benjamin had stolen it.

Stolen treasure

When the cup was found in the sack the brothers were distraught. They couldn't leave Benjamin behind. They knew that it would kill Jacob, to lose another son. So they returned to Joseph's palace.

Joseph said that Benjamin should be his slave. One brother, Judah pleaded with Joseph to free Benjamin and take him as a slave instead.

Changed hearts!

Joseph now knew that God had changed the hearts of his brothers. They were different men.

Who is who?

Jacob: Father of Joseph and Benjamin and their brothers.
Rachael: Joseph and Benjamin's mother.
Leah: Jacob's other wife.
Jacob's twelves sons: Reuben, Simeon, Levi, Judah, Issachar, Zebulun; Gad; Asher; Joseph; Benjamin; Dan and Naphtali.

He broke down in tears. Turning to his brothers he exclaimed, 'I am Joseph who you sold into slavery. Do not be angry with yourselves for it was all part of God's plan to save lives. God sent me here to save your lives from the famine.'

What a reunion that was! We all congratulate Joseph on finding his family once again. We wish them all the very best during their stay in Egypt.

An emotional reunion between Joseph and his brothers.

NEWS FLASH

A report has just come in that Joseph has invited his whole family to come and live with him in Egypt. Pharaoh himself has granted them permission to take their wives and children and to set up home in our country. Who knows what will happen now... we wish Joseph and his family all the best for the future.

Thought for the day

It is good to think on the things which the Bible tells us to do. Here are some things to think about as you go out and about today.

The Lord sees everything that is happening everywhere; he is watching us whether we do good or do evil. Proverbs 15:3

Trust in the Lord with all your heart. Never rely on what you think you know. Proverbs 3:5

From the Editor

At first, things went well for the Israelites in Egypt, but it didn't stay that way. One day, a new Pharaoh came to the throne who had no knowledge of Joseph and what he had done for the country of Egypt. The Israelites soon found themselves slaves to the Egyptian people. But as we have seen in the previous articles the one true God was there to help them.

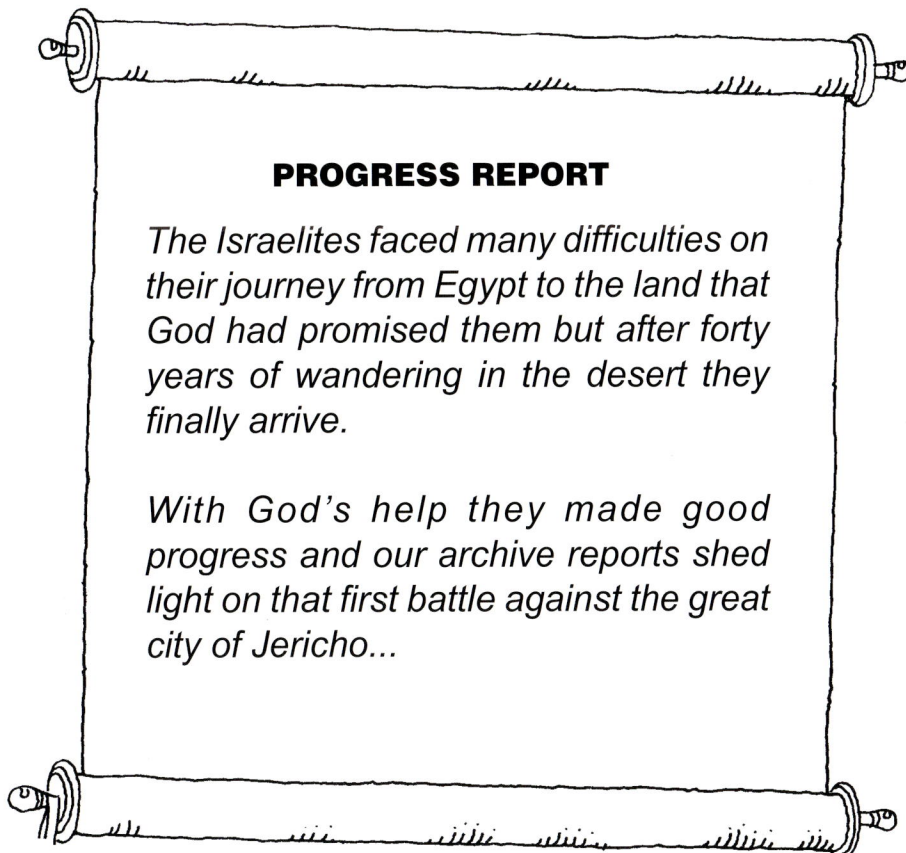

PROGRESS REPORT

The Israelites faced many difficulties on their journey from Egypt to the land that God had promised them but after forty years of wandering in the desert they finally arrive.

With God's help they made good progress and our archive reports shed light on that first battle against the great city of Jericho...

Walls come tumbling down

The great city of Jericho is in ruins, the huge defensive walls have fallen down. There is chaos everywhere.

The Israelites destroy everything

It is quite incredible because this was one of the most secure and tightly guarded cities in the region. The people of Jericho knew the Israelites might attack at any time. The Israelites had been camped outside the city for many days. Now it has happened. Current reports say that the Israelites have destroyed everything in the city. There has been much confusion and other reports say that one family has survived. As we go to print we are trying to confirm this report. More details in our next issue.

Survivor story told

We now print two survivor stories from this tragic event.

After Moses died on top of mount Nebo Joshua became leader. He lead the Israelites over the river Jordan to attack God's enemies.

God spoke to Joshua and told him that the Israelites would defeat Jericho. He told Joshua to get all the armed men to march around Jericho once a day for six days. Seven priests carrying horns were to march in front of the ark of the covenant (a sacred golden chest that God had instructed Moses to build. God's law was kept inside it.) On day seven they were to march around seven times with the priests blowing their trumpets. When the horns gave a long blast on that day, all the people were to shout, the walls would fall down and the people were to run into the city. They carried the plan out just as they had been told and the walls all came down. The destruction was amazing. They destroyed

Spies on the roof!

everything ... except for one family... the family of Rahab, she tells her story here.

"Two Israelite spies came to my house and the king's men came looking for them. I hid the spies on the roof under the stalks of flax. When night came I let them out of a window in the city wall and lowered them gently down with a rope. 'Run to the hills' I urged them, 'Hide for three days until the king's men give up looking for you.' I knew God would let the Israelites take over the city so I pleaded with the spies to make sure that my family and

I were kept safe. 'As long as you tell no one about us you will not be harmed,' they said. As a sign they gave me a scarlet cord. 'When the attack comes hang this cord out of your window. The people in your house will then be safe.'

When the great day came, we watched the marching

Rahab helps spies escape.

round the city. It went on and on and we knew the attack would come soon.

Crash! Bang! Yell!

Suddenly trumpets blew and there was crashing and banging and yelling as the walls began to fall. People were fighting all around and I waited to be rescued. Joshua remembered the spies' promise. As the noise and racket of the battle went on round about us my family and I were all led out of the city, to safety."

What a story! It reminds us that to follow God is the best thing to do.

Small Boy wins over Big Man

An amazing incident has been brought to our attention. The Philistine army had gathered near Judah. They were ready to fight the Israelites. The Philistines had a huge man on their side - a giant, and he wore amazing armour, nothing could get at him. His name was Goliath. No Israelite man would fight him.

Goliath!

At that time a young lad called David appeared at the Israelite camp. David's brothers were in the army so he had to give them some food and then come home and tell his father how they were getting on. Normally he looked after sheep, but not today. His day out would turn him into a hero. Read on to find out how.

Who will fight the giant?

After arriving at the camp he found his brothers. While he was talking to them, they heard Goliath calling, wanting someone to fight him.

David asked what was going on and when it was all explained to him, he said that he would go and fight the giant. David's brothers couldn't believe it and when the king heard of it neither could he.

They all told David that he was just a boy while Goliath was an experienced fighter.

David reminded them that while looking after his fathers sheep he had had to fight off a lion and a bear. He had done this with power from God.

David believed that God's power would help him now,

Power from God

because Goliath was an enemy of God's people. Well the king even gave David his own armour but it was no use, David had never worn armour before. He took it all off and instead, took his staff, his sling and five smooth pebbles from the stream. The Philistines looked on in amazement and disgust. Goliath would soon sort this young boy out. They forgot in whose power David came. David called out and reminded them that he came in the name and power of the Lord. David put a pebble in his sling, and slung it at Goliath. Goliath collapsed in a heap. David had triumphed over the Philistines by the power of God. Young David was taken to live with the king from then on. Quite something for such a young lad to do, but it reminds us all what the power of God can do.

David chooses his stones.

STRANGE MEAL FOR BIG FISH

Read this incredible story. Can you imagine being inside a fish and still being alive after three days? It seems impossible, but we have discovered a story that tells us that it is indeed possible - because of God.

Usually visitors to Nineveh arrive in ships or by road however we have had another visitor, Jonah, a servant of the most high God, who travelled to our shores in the stomach of a rather large fish.

Jonah had been told by God to go to a place called Nineveh and tell the people there about God because they were very bad and did not follow Gods ways. Jonah did not want to go so he set off in the other direction for a place called Tarshish. He tried to get away from God but as we will see no one can do that. To get to Tarshish Jonah had to travel by boat. As the journey got under way a huge storm blew up and everyone was terrified and they began to throw cargo overboard to make the ship lighter and prevent sinking. Everyone was terrified except for Jonah, he

Fish Report:

It was -

" Huge "
" Colossal "
" VERY BIG "

had gone below deck and had fallen asleep. Eventually the captain of the ship went and woke Jonah and asked him to pray for safety. Meanwhile the sailors spoke to Jonah and decided that he was the cause of the trouble. Jonah told them to throw him overboard into the raging sea as that was what he deserved for not obeying God.

The fish spat Jonah out!

They tried to row to shore but could not manage it so in the end they threw Jonah into the water. However all was not lost for Jonah. God sent a fish at just the right time and the fish swallowed Jonah up. Jonah was stuck here for the next three days. He prayed to God for forgiveness. After three days and nights the fish spat Jonah out onto dry land. Again God spoke to Jonah and told him to go to Nineveh.

This time Jonah obeyed. When he arrived he told the people the message from God. Nineveh would be destroyed in forty days if they did not leave their

Jonah is spat out onto dry land.

evil ways and follow God. They were terrified. The king ordered everyone to pray for forgiveness. God heard them and decided not to punish them. The city was saved!!

MAN SURVIVES NIGHT WITH LIONS

It hardly seems possible that the story here could be true, and yet it is. Our reporter is glad that he did not have to go right to the scene of the events in order to make his report.

'Not a scratch!'

A young man called Daniel has just been taken out of a lions den after spending a night there - without a scratch! The lions made no attempt to attack him and were perfectly gentle. It all came about because Daniel would not follow the king's command. The command said that people were only allowed to pray to the king. Daniel was respected by the king but would only pray to the one true God. Some of the king's wise men did not like

Daniel: Safe and sound and not a scratch!

Daniel and they tricked the king into passing this new law about prayer. When Daniel continued to pray to his God - the wise men reported him to the king. Then the king realised what was going on. However as he had agreed to the new law himself there was nothing he could do. He had no choice but to carry out